IT'S TIME TO EAT EDAMAME

It's Time to Eat EDAMAME

Walter the Educator

Silent King Books
A WhichHead Entertainment Imprint

Copyright © 2025 by Walter the Educator

All rights reserved. No part of this book may be reproduced in any manner whatsoever without written per- mission except in the case of brief quotations embodied in critical articles and reviews.

First Printing, 2024

Disclaimer

This book is a literary work; the story is not about specific persons, locations, situations, and/or circumstances unless mentioned in a historical context. Any resemblance to real persons, locations, situations, and/or circumstances is coincidental. This book is for entertainment and informational purposes only. The author and publisher offer this information without warranties expressed or implied. No matter the grounds, neither the author nor the publisher will be accountable for any losses, injuries, or other damages caused by the reader's use of this book. The use of this book acknowledges an understanding and acceptance of this disclaimer.

It's Time to Eat EDAMAME is a collectible early learning book by Walter the Educator suitable for all ages belonging to Walter the Educator's Time to Eat Book Series. Collect more books at WaltertheEducator.com

USE THE EXTRA SPACE TO TAKE NOTES AND DOCUMENT YOUR MEMORIES

EDAMAME

It's time to eat, hooray, hooray!

It's Time to Eat
Edamame

Edamame's on the way!

Little beans so green and bright,

A tasty snack that feels just right!

Pick a pod and hold it tight,

Give a squeeze, oh, what a sight!

Pop! The beans jump out so quick,

Into my mouth, so fun to pick!

Soft and chewy, small and round,

A yummy taste, a happy sound!

Salty, nutty, fresh, and neat,

Edamame's fun to eat!

Steam them hot or eat them cool,

A perfect snack for home or school!

Dip in sauce or eat them plain,

One by one or all the same!

It's Time to Eat
Edamame

Crunch, crunch, munch, munch,

I could eat them for my lunch!

Or at dinner, side by side,

With rice and fish, so fun to try!

Tiny beans with power inside,

They help me run, they help me ride!

Strong and happy, big and bright,

Edamame makes me feel just right!

Grandma loves them, Mom does too,

Even Grandpa says, "Woohoo!"

We all sit and share a plate,

Edamame tastes so great!

One more pod, let's have some more,

They're so fun, I just adore!

Eating beans, so soft and sweet,

It's Time to Eat Edamame

A special snack that can't be beat!

Let's all share and eat them fast,

This little treat is sure to last!

One, two, three, then maybe four,

I think I'll grab a few more!

Now they're gone, oh no, oh dear!

We'll have more again next year!

Edamame's fresh and fun to see,

It's Time to Eat
Edamame

A perfect snack for you and me!

ABOUT THE CREATOR

Walter the Educator is one of the pseudonyms for Walter Anderson. Formally educated in Chemistry, Business, and Education, he is an educator, an author, a diverse entrepreneur, and he is the son of a disabled war veteran. "Walter the Educator" shares his time between educating and creating. He holds interests and owns several creative projects that entertain, enlighten, enhance, and educate, hoping to inspire and motivate you. Follow, find new works, and stay up to date with Walter the Educator™ at WaltertheEducator.com

www.ingramcontent.com/pod-product-compliance
Lightning Source LLC
LaVergne TN
LVHW010622070526
838199LV00063BA/5247